# The Captain's Garden

## A REFLECTIVE JOURNEY HOME THROUGH THE ART OF
## PAUL LANDRY

EDITED BY BETTY BALLANTINE
THE GREENWICH WORKSHOP, INC.

# The Captain's Garden

## A REFLECTIVE JOURNEY HOME THROUGH THE ART OF

## PAUL LANDRY

## *I dedicate this book to my family*

Thank you, Joe, for printing my stories for me whenever I asked. You managed to fit
them into your busy schedule, and I appreciate that. Your comments were great, especially
the funny ones. I admire your talent, Joe; thank you for using it to help me write this book.

Thank you, Hope, for being my delightful model. As you look at your pink beret,
*Christmas Treasures* and *Sunshine and Flowers*, you'll see what an inspiration you are to me.
When you see us skating together, hand in hand, remember: you'll always be my favorite skating
partner. Hope, your beautiful smile and sweet spirit always sing a lovely song in my heart.

Thank you, Tom, for your happy and instant reply of "Okay, Dad" whenever I needed a paperboy,
a boy with a hoop, a band member or even a grocer's helper. I'll always admire your patience, Tom: while
I'd be thinking of yet another prop or location, you'd still be holding a pose. When you saw the finished painting of
*Joseph's Corner*, you didn't seem to mind that I had painted his helper with your yo-yo in his pocket. Or did I?

For Mary: For the encouragement and loving, helping hands that made this book come true.

To each of you, my collectors: Thank you for welcoming me into your home.

To the coach and every member of his creative team: My heartfelt appreciation for yet another work of art.

A GREENWICH WORKSHOP PRESS BOOK
Copyright © 1996 The Greenwich Workshop, Inc.
All rights reserved. No part of this book may be reproduced, altered, trimmed, laminated,
mounted or combined with any text or image to produce any form of definitive work. Nor may
any part of this book be transmitted in any form or by any means, electronic or mechanical, including
photocopying and recording, or by any information storage and retrieval system, without permission in writing
from the publisher. The images in this book, and the entire book, are protected under the Copyright
Law, and the publisher will prosecute to the full extent of the law any unauthorized use of them.
Inquiries should be addressed to The Greenwich Workshop, Inc.,
One Greenwich Place, P.O. Box 875, Shelton, Connecticut 06484-0875.
Distributed to the trade by Artisan, A Division of Workman Publishing, 708 Broadway, New York, NY 10003

•

*Library of Congress Cataloging-in-Publication Data:*
Landry, Paul A.    The captain's garden : a reflective journey home
through the art of Paul Landry / [edited by Betty Ballantine].
p.   cm.    ISBN 0-86713-033-4 (hardcover : alk. paper).
1. Landry, Paul A.    2. Painters—United States—Biography.
3. Impressionism (Art)—United States.  I. Ballantine, Betty.  II. Title.
ND237.L267A2    1996    759. 13—dc20    [B]    96-14092

•

For information about the limited edition prints, fine art lithography and canvas prints of
Paul Landry, please write to The Greenwich Workshop, Inc., at the above address, or call (800) 241-2171
(in the U.S.) to be connected with the authorized Greenwich Workshop dealer nearest you.

FRONTIS ART
2–3  Detail from *The Brass Ring*
4–5  Detail from *Summer Mist*
6–7  Detail from *Autumn Market*

•

Edited by Betty Ballantine
Book design by Judy Turziano and Peter J. Landa
Display typeface, *Wilderness*, by Philip Bouwsma
Manufactured in Singapore by Toppan
First Edition
96  97  98    0  9  8  7  6  5  4  3  2  1

# Contents

## Cottage by the Sea

*(Detail) Beside the bay is a little cottage, cozied in by a picket fence with an arbor. The flowers burst with color and beauty all summer long, while the water reflects the multi-blue shades of the sky.*

# Introduction

The art of seeing is an essential talent for an artist. It provides the host of impressions from which, at the appropriate time, the artist can call upon one that he chooses to re-create. Paul Landry's magic lies in combining these reflections into thoughtfully fashioned compositions. They are visual short stories of color, familiarity and emotion.

Paul Landry invites us to enter and experience an endless realm of peace and beauty, where his art beckons not only the eye, but the heart as well. The calm power of his artistry has created for us a world in which reality takes on a life of its own. It lifts our spirits and transcends the limits of time and place. This sanctuary is *The Captain's Garden*.

Here one has the impression of hearing the chiming of church bells on a village green or the flourish of a small bird's wings in a flower-strewn yard; the murmur of summertime crowds in the background of a seaside boardwalk or the slice of a skater's blade across an ice-bound wintertime bay. It is a place where soft breezes are laden with the fragrances of blossoming trees and flowers as they mingle with the ocean air.

Many of Paul Landry's paintings reflect impressions from his childhood in Nova Scotia, where he spent his youth close to the sea. There he not only met the fishermen who frequent his scenes, his studies and vignettes (little gems that his collectors treasure), but took to the ocean with them as well. His affinity for life in the country and the splendor of nature, and a passion for the simple pace in life come from here as well.

It is these memories from the early days, along with details imagined by the artist, that enliven his paintings. Roadways slope down to calm harbors where schooners rest near a farther shore; pathways lead through beds of flowers to mysterious backgrounds; New England cottages, doorways and Victorian-trimmed verandahs house the community in which we wish we could live.

The artist's palette works magic with light. Sharp, crisp colors give the impression of a balmy summer afternoon or a frosty winter's morn. Translucent tones create an evening sky that still holds the light of a departed sun, or make the ice glow gray beneath the low horizon of a cloudy late-afternoon sky. Flower shops or picturesque streets burst forth in an opulent spectrum rivaled only by nature herself.

Paul tries to evoke in his work a peace and tranquillity that, while we seem to be able to place it, eludes us. Sometimes his figures are clothed as if in a scene from years ago, yet familiar today. A country lane may be like the ones traveled recently, but replaced with dirt. A horse and wagon, coach or sleigh may play a part in his pictures as well, adding an air of days gone by.

Paul's mother, an avid and award-winning gardener, lies at the heart of his fascination with florals. As a boy, he admired and was inspired by what she could do with her garden, though he was set to work mostly in his father's vegetable garden. Today he spends much of his leisure time creating and tending the flower gardens of his own home. This could easily be considered "research," absorbing the impressions of his surroundings for future compositions.

The more-than-casual observer will recognize the artist's constant use of his family's names—Joseph, Hope, Thomas and their mother, Mary, in his art. Even his pets frequent his work. In some places, the people themselves appear, since the entire family is part of his creative process.

Strong feelings of family and community can be found in Paul's work. These are further accented by his joy of celebration. Pure exhilaration is expressed in the excitement of his crowds on seaside holidays or the sparkling, subtle tones of reflected winter light as a town gathers to skate on a frozen river. The Christmas spirit lives within his paintings.

Come and step joyfully into this magical world, the nostalgic realm of artist Paul Landry.

*Floral Cherub*
*(Detail) A garden angel contemplates the coming day while enjoying heaven's blossom-borne scent.*

# Halcyon Days

We had a
wonderful life in
St. Margaret's Bay,
just ideal for
growing up.

# Halcyon Days

*Harbor Lane*
*(Detail) After a day at sea, a sailor returns to his sunlit cottage on a well-worn lane. The picket fences and the flowers that spill over them welcome him back, as they welcome all who pass by in this seaside setting.*

The farmhouse would now be nearly 150 years old. It easily took the strongest bay winds and even harder blows from the North Atlantic and beyond. The beams of the house were hand-hewn, mortised and wooden-pegged. The floors and most of the walls were made from pine boards while the ceiling and some walls were plaster over lath, the plaster mixed with mohair or horsehair to strengthen it. A massive central chimney with four fireplaces anchored the structure.

In the kitchen there were brick ovens for baking. In front of these stood a large, shiny, black and chrome wood-burning stove. The pride of the house, it was polished on a regular basis. It was used not only for cooking, but for heating as well. Hot water was always waiting in the kettle for making a cup of tea. Steep, steep steps led from the kitchen and front hall to the upstairs, where there were four rooms for sleeping. The front of the house overlooked the bay, facing west. It was high enough on a hill to watch ninety-degree sunsets and the radiant after-glow that lasted long after the sun had gone down. There was a Victorian sunken garden with cultured and wild roses, peonies and more. The vegetable garden was huge.

Today, the cinnamon aroma of a freshly baked apple pie, a warm bowl of fish chowder or the moist nasal sting of a winter's morning never fails to send me back to our farm on St. Margaret's Bay.

# ST. MARGARET'S BAY

St. Margaret's Bay is located in the central part of Nova Scotia, Canada. It's about twenty miles southwest of Halifax, my hometown. The bay is about seven miles wide, with a twenty-mile shoreline. It's a charming bay, with fishing villages, beaches, coves and out islands just waiting to be explored. Fishing and farming are the main occupations, and most of the people around there do both.

I grew up at the end of the Depression and during the Second World War. Halifax was a very busy city, and its harbor was a point of embarkation for convoys heading for Europe. It was fairly safe as cities go, but my dad, having lived through the explosions of two ships in Halifax Harbor (one, an ammunition ship that leveled half the city), thought that having a place in the country would be a lot safer and, moreover, the air would be cleaner and the grass greener. He also thought that he and his wife, along with the seven children, would enjoy summertime living in the country. For himself, he wanted to continue his active lifestyle—he was a former athletic champ and current athletic director for the

*Bayview*
*On top of the hill, behind the farm, was the place to be for a breath-taking view.*

### St. Margaret's Bay

*My summer home in Nova Scotia. This wonderful old farm's flowers were lovingly tended by Dad's Agnes Marie, my mum. Her skill with flowers was the envy of all around. She was especially known for her roses.*

Halifax school system—and figured country life would offer him a splendid opportunity to work a large vegetable garden, while our mum could indulge her love of flower-gardening.

The farm my father found and fell in love with was ideal. It had fifty acres of land surrounding a Cape-style home high on the hill overlooking the bay, and an additional fifty wooded acres for hunting and berry-picking. The land ran right down to the bay, where beaches and rocky inlets invited exploration. Adjoining this land was a fishing village, with fishermen's cottages and work shacks that led to the docks, where sailboats and motorboats were moored.

As for buying this paradise, at first my father found it too costly. He

was deeply disappointed, but Dad had great faith. Now, I wouldn't say that he was responsible, but as he hoped and prayed for an alternative, the seas off New England produced a hurricane. Out of nowhere it came, up the coast and into the bay—one of the worst, they said. It uprooted trees, flattened barns, lifted roofs and carried away a few chicken coops as it continued on to wherever it is that hurricanes go.

After the storm, my father anxiously returned to look at his paradise again. Except for a collapsed barn and a few shingles missing from the house, it had withstood the hurricane. The owner, however, hadn't fared as well and was suddenly more willing to negotiate. After some short bargaining, the farm was his.

*Harbor Lane*
*(Left) Dazzling views are found above the harbor, where sunlight bathes the well-worn lane.*

*Sailor's Garden*
*A sailor, off at sea, knows his garden waits to welcome him home once more.*

# THE COUNTRY LIFE

We had a wonderful life in St. Margaret's Bay, ideal for kids growing up. The summers and winters were filled with excitement, challenge, work and a lot of fun. Those years in the country are the ones I'll always remember.

The farm's vegetable garden was huge. All of us worked at weeding and harvesting. We each had to put in an average of three hours a day; the rest of the time was ours. Berries were my specialty, and we had tons of them. There were sweet, juicy strawberries; raspberries, both red and black; foxberries and blueberries. I remember our mum giving us huge containers to fill for her. The blueberries were as tiny as could be, and it would take tons of them to fill a bucket. My dad used to tell us that the berries in the country were so big that it would take just one to make a pie. Well, I believed him and wondered about it, but I never found one. Still, I always finished first. Mum never told me she didn't want sticks and leaves in with the berries.

No matter how many chores we had to do, we always found time to discover things we hadn't seen before. There was even time to make our own things to play with, as well as learn something new each day. There was the orchard, great for its tart-sweet

*Homeside Garden*
*If summer harmony is an abundant mixture of sea, sunshine and flowers, this harborside home is blessed with the sweetest of music.*

apples. It had a huge rock wall surrounding it, across the top of which we would make daredevil runs. Sometimes we'd build treehouses—a few of which required a password at the foot of the tree. We'd play ball, go fishing and enjoy it all. Wherever we went, the dog would tag along.

It was glorious when we stayed over for autumn and winter. The home we were to move into in Halifax wasn't ready to be lived in, so we experienced more than just a country summer. Even after school started, the fun didn't stop. The school was just one room, and Mrs. Covey taught all grade levels. Autumn meant apple pies, and Mum must have baked hundreds, maybe more— enough anyway so that all her preserving and baking carried us through till spring.

### Summer Buddies

*Soon there will be two more free spirits of summer—once the flowers are sold, that is. The memories of these summertime enterprises— flower sales, paper routes, lemonade stands or fishing in the bay—are among my favorites.*

### Apple Orchard

*We loved being barefoot all summer long. As we walked the rock walls and explored the orchard's paths, its trees seemed to be holding out their arms, beckoning for us to climb and have a seat, even if just for a minute.*

When winter came, the shovel was part of your regular gear, like your skates and books. That way, it didn't matter how much snow fell; you just took your shovel and shoveled till you got there. We'd skate away our recess time, then slip and slide back home to build snow forts in defensible places all over the hills. Christmas was extra special that first winter.

In St. Margaret's Bay, our whole world had expanded. Our horizons were wider, and the potential for fun and excitement was endless. At the same time, we shared in a community that was much more personal than any we'd experienced before. That's life, I guess, whether you're raised on a farm or in the city. But in memory, the country certainly seems the best place for growing up.

**Orchard Hill**
(Detail) We played
hide-and-seek, leap-
frog and other games,
devouring apples along
the way. We would run
and play till late in the
afternoon, when we
would hear the dinner
bell ring. On the way
home, we'd already be
making plans for the
next day.

## CAPTAIN KIDD AND A
## WHALE OF A TALE

The bay next to St. Margaret's Bay is Mahone Bay. On the southern point of that is the town of Lunenburg. Lunenburg is famous for its fishing schooners and boatbuilding. In the bay is Oak Island, the legendary resting place of Captain Kidd's treasures. For the last eighty years or so, the island has been abused by continuous digging. Some evidence

has been found, but no treasures. Living so close to this island and hearing the stories so often filled our hearts with hopes and dreams of adventure and finding a chest full of gold.

One summer, I had a small rowboat that I rigged with a sail. With my brother, I ventured out into St. Margaret's Bay to a small island. Instantly we became pirates of old. We looked for or pretended to be burying treasure chests full of booty from passing sailing ships that I imagined we'd boarded in our bay.

That summer was unusually hot. One day, hundreds of pilot whales

*Summer Afternoon*
*The old harbor has lots of history,*
*and the little village is delightful.*
*But for this afternoon, fishing from*
*their schooner, these boys find all*
*they need in the sea.*

*Bluenose Country*
(Previous pages) Lunenburg was home to the
fastest schooner ever built, the "Bluenose."

*A New Dawn*
(Above) Down at the dock, the dawn
announces the arrival of a new morning
in a harbor rich with pride and heritage.
This captures the atmosphere of a
time past.

appeared. They were following and feeding on squid as the warm cur-
rents of the Gulf Stream moved closer to the shore. It was an incredible
sight. The whales were so close together that you could almost walk
across the bay on their backs. I remember hearing that one boat was
lifted right out of the water when a whale beneath it surfaced to spout.
The largest whale seen was about twenty feet long and weighed at least
two tons. Fishing was suspended. Even our neighbor Raymond, the Paul
Bunyan of the Bay, wouldn't venture out there.

However, boys will be boys, so my friend Ralph and I, fearless knights
of the bay who needed no armor, rowed out in my small boat to see the

whales close-up. We rowed after one and, as he surfaced, reached out to touch him with the oar. Captain Ahab would have been proud enough to hire us. As we watched them swim under the boat and breach on either side, we'd shout, "Thar she blows!" Oh, how we wished to hold on to a gigantic fluke and go for a Nantucket sleigh ride. Eventually we rowed back to the protection of the cove.

I couldn't wait to get home and tell Mum what fun we'd had among the whales that afternoon. That's something I shouldn't have done, as I spent the next two days on the woodpile, splitting wood. I noticed that Ralph wasn't around, either. I doubt that Captain Ahab was similarly beached.

*Bringing Home the Tree*
*(Detail) A special time to be together: blankets of snow cover trees and ground, smoke from the chimney curls through the air and soon they will be home trimming the tree.*

# Bayside Reflections

My marine
characters are those
dear old fishermen
who were my
teachers of the sea.

# Bayside Reflections

## Reflections

*(Detail) In the harbor of a seaside village, cargo and fishing schooners dry their sails, and seine boats drift with the tide. The combination of the two is a long-vanished sight, reminiscent of the coastline where I grew up and of fishing villages the world over.*

Before iron ships, Nova Scotia was known for building wooden fishing vessels—from large schooners, like the champion *Bluenose*, for use on the Grand Banks of the Atlantic, to the smaller sloops and cape boats that fished the calm water like St. Margaret's Bay. They were designed to be fast, both to return for processing and for the fact that the first back got the higher price. It was hard to find someone who was not in some way tied to the sea.

Life in St. Margaret's Bay was certainly tied to the sea and was a life for the hearty and robust. It created an environment that not only built character, but bred characters as well. For a child, in both summer and winter, it was a wonderland. The days of boats driven entirely by sail had passed, but there were still schooners with sail about, sturdy enough to cope with the gales of the Atlantic. When the storms of winter brought on snow and ice, hats, scarves and mittens ensured that life didn't skip a beat.

Winter meant Christmas, which may have been the highlight of that time of year. But the bay became such a wonderland then, with its snow, frozen ponds and inlets, that it simply created a whole new world in which we as children could play. Even the bright, freezing, sunlit days reflected the warmth of family and community that filled our hearts and homes.

# THE FISHERMAN

Raymond, our neighbor, lived in a cottage left to him by his aunt. He was a fisherman, which alone was pretty special, but he also had a way of doing things that were, well, beyond the norm. It seemed that Raymond received a message from God telling him to build a sturdy boat in that fine cottage. With a twenty-pound persuader and a crowbar, he gutted the interior. In the kitchen he built a blacksmith's shop with a bellows and an anvil. We watched in fascination through that fall and winter as Raymond built his boat.

In September, he laid a thirty-foot keel that went from wall to wall. Lumber was passed in through the windows. Day by day, the boat became larger and larger, and actually started to fill the cottage. Soon we began to notice certain difficulties in the relationship of the boat to the door. We began asking questions. Raymond always had an answer: "We'll grease the sides and slide it out the door," or "I'll take it apart and put it together outside again."

At last, the boat was caulked and painted. It looked absolutely

*Entertaining Gulls*
*(Above) The eager sounds of the gulls reflect their thanks as the fishermen share their catch of the day.*

## Harborside
(Left) This three-masted schooner is similar to the one my grandfather sailed. These ships would carry lumber from Nova Scotia down the New England coast and return filled with provisions.

## The Yellow Slicker
Hardy gear was the call of the day for the men of the fleet.

*Mary Hope in Her Pink Beret*

## Cecilia

*I can picture my grandmother Cecilia as a young wife and mother, enjoying the afternoon by the water with her first-born. Perhaps they talked of when Papa would be returning from the sea and his life as a captain. In her beautiful life of ninety-nine years, she became the mother of thirteen. The last two were twins, one of whom was my father, Joseph.*

## Seaside Gems

*(Detail) A family strolls beside the ocean, awaiting their sailor's return.*

### Afternoon Swim
*It was a golden world for the fishermen's sons at dockside. The sea was a place of plenty as well as a place of play.*

beautiful, but the day of reckoning was coming. It was spring, the fishing season was about to start, and Raymond needed that boat from the house. One fine day, Raymond appeared with a team of oxen, his brother and a couple of fishermen. We believed that no matter how much grease he put on the sides of the boat, there was no way he was going to slide it out the door. Other interested fishing folks from the village started to gather around.

Now, with the proper audience to appreciate his ingenuity, Raymond took out his reliable persuader and crowbar and simply tore down the whole side of the cottage. We couldn't believe our eyes! He hooked the oxen team to the stern, pulled the boat over rolling logs down the hill and launched it into the water. As he sailed out of sight, we could hear the proud captain shout, "There'll be a blankety-blank party for all the blankety-blanks here tonight!" What a day, what a party! Raymond was quite the sport, and everyone loved him that way.

## Orange Dory
(Above) A dory on a schooner was a fisherman's best friend. Often they were orange for easy recognition at sea.

## Sail-Maker's Wagon
It was never too early to mend a sail. After all, a stitch in time saves nine.

[42]

# FISHING

Naturally, my first fishing adventure was with Raymond. I was twelve and so excited that I slept little the night before. I had no trouble making the four A.M. sailing time. With the distinctive putt-putt of the one-cylinder engine echoing off both sides of the cove, we headed out into the calm waters of the bay.

In shallower water, about a mile out, we pulled in Raymond's preset gill net. Raymond chose this spot for herring. Hand over hand, we pulled it from the water. Even though it was dark, the herring still glistened as we took them aboard. Farther out, in the middle of the bay, Raymond checked his trawl-line. Similar to a clothesline, though much longer and set with hooks and bait, it had been placed in these deeper waters the day before. Mostly, one would catch haddock and cod this way.

Soon, though, we headed on to the mouth of the bay, where the rocky, shallow banks provided the best fishing. Many other boats from the different villages around the bay had already arrived, and the men were hand-line fishing from the sides of their sloops. I'll always remember that sight: the rising sun and how its light was so magnificent on the boats and on the water.

Though it was very calm, it seemed to me that the swells were

*Harbor Glow*
*(Left) Life beside the sea could never help but to impress upon one how peaceful were the effects of harmony and color.*

*Shooting the Sun*
*A foul-weather-clad captain fixes his position with a read on the noonday sun.*

### Shades of Blue
*The mingling of mist from the sea and the midday sun was a common sight on the shoreline. Here, daylight finally breaks through in a palette of harbor colors.*

ten feet high. The waves would crest and lower into troughs like passing through mountains and valleys. One moment you were on top of the world, and in a flash you'd disappear into the shadows of the crest. The boats around you a second ago would be gone. It was the most exhilarating feeling I had ever experienced. It was like seeing the sun come up every ten seconds, a joyous rise of magic light endlessly repeated! All the while that this was going on, we were hand-lining, pulling up cod and haddock as fast as we could dump them into the boat. This is strenuous work, and my hands were raw by the time the boat was full and we headed home.

The trip in had to be done quickly, as we had no ice to chill the fish. We arrived back by mid-morning, and Raymond filleted some of the haddock, which he gave to me. I put it in a pail and ran up the hill to our house. My mum immediately panfried it, and it was the best ever. I had worked for it with the men I had come to admire.

That was the first of almost daily trips each season. I'll always be thankful for those experiences, and now, when I paint them, I'm again on those boats. My marine characters are real, those wonderful old fishermen who were my teachers as I grew up by the sea.

# A CANADIAN CHRISTMAS

Christmas when I was growing up in Canada was lots of wonderful things. First, it was cold. It was cold from October through April first or so. Therefore, freezing weather in December was a given. We searched the woods near our home for our tree. When we got it down to two favorites, we would cut them both down. The winners, at least from our point of view, were dragged home. One was chosen to be trimmed, and the sunroom would be its new home. We strung lights of all colors around it and covered the branches with plenty of tinsel. The other tree was used for our manger, the mantel, outside decorations and anywhere else that a touch of green would enhance that Christmas feeling.

*Wintered In*
*A pair of fishermen's vessels, already partway through the long winter, have two months till spring, and then it's anchors aweigh.*

My mum hung the ornaments with great reverence and respect. Each was precious. Some were treasured because her children had made them. Others brought special memories and a smile to her lips or a tear to her eye. The stories that she told about them made the tree all the more beautiful. Long before Christmas, we had looked through the Sears catalogue and filled our eyes and heads with things that we hoped Santa would bring. When Christmas Eve finally arrived, the big, curtained double doors to the sunroom were closed.

On Christmas Day, we got up early and went to church. An anxious breakfast followed, and as soon as we were finished, my dad brought each of us into the sunroom, one by one. We had to promise to keep our eyes closed as tight as they could be, until we were each put in our special places to stand. Of course, no peeking was allowed.

At the count of three, we could open our eyes and see what

*Cove Skaters*
*(Above) During the deepest chills of winter, even the saltwater bays would freeze over, creating a Canadian wonderland.*

*Christmas at Mystic Seaport*
*Sharing in the warm spirit of the season, the moonlight glows in the crisp air of this famous Connecticut port.*

Santa had brought. You never saw happier kids. Mum was always knitting, so we each got a scarf, hat, mittens, socks or a sweater. They were always nice and warm. In no time, we were outside trying out all of our new things. Late in the afternoon, we had our holiday turkey and all the trimmings. Dessert was always plum pudding. Special holiday cookies, made by Mum and my sisters, rounded out the choice of treats we had that day. Later, looking at and listening to the big logs crackling in the fireplace, we'd sing Christmas carols.

All through the holidays, neighbors stopped by for tea and sweets, and we would do the same. There was the visit to Lady Lucy, who always hung the gifts she had received on her tree. My brothers and I tried very hard not to burst out laughing when we saw all her new underwear hanging from the branches. We were kind of embarrassed and somewhat curious as only boys can be when they are nine, eleven and thirteen years old. We couldn't wait to visit the following year.

Before the new year arrived, we always had a taffy pull in our kitchen. It's a wonder we didn't lose our teeth trying to chew it. Sometimes we'd roast peanuts or potatoes in the fireplace. They were tasty treats, but mostly these were fun things to do together. The whole winter had so much to offer us: the snow, storms, fort-building, skating, sleigh-riding and hockey. But above all, Christmas was the best.

*Christmas Treasures*
*(Previous pages)*
*Sharing is Christmas's most beautiful tradition. This little one is bringing her treasures to some extra-special people in her life.*

*A Canadian Christmas*
*(Far right) Red-cheeked and heading home, these boys will soon be gathering around a warm hearth, sipping mulled cider and lending their voices to Christmas song.*

*Cape Cod Sleigh Ride*
*Can't you can just hear the sleigh bells ring as the horses pull this cutter through the countryside?*

# Verdant Memories

The sound was music to my ears. The faster I ran, the better the music.

# Verdant Memories

*Joseph's Corner*
*(Detail) The social aspect*
*of country life revolves*
*around four main places:*
*home, church, school and*
*the country store. At the*
*store, you could find milk,*
*homemade bread, fresh*
*eggs, candy and even*
*mousetraps. The grocer's*
*boy helped you with your*
*bags, and he might even*
*teach you a yo-yo trick or*
*two if you were interested.*

In retrospect, our lives give me the impression of coming together like an English garden. At first look, it is a ramshackle jumble of people, places and events forming in the haphazard patchwork of seeds that were apparently randomly sewn. However, upon closer inspection, an order and rhythm can begin to be seen, and there emerge patterns indicating the underlying tending of the garden's growth.

A world of influences acts upon the garden. Family ties and traditions will determine the seeds that will grow to begin with, as well as the way that they are laid out. With great care and love, nice, neat rows and patches are planned, but seemingly innocuous events can forever alter their formation. Climates change, drought deprives, and storms threaten the garden. For each of these, though, there is a season of bounty provided in return.

Childhood chores can become lifelong passions; a paper route leads to an apprenticeship and a career in art. Visitors come and go, some simply enjoying a little time in the garden with no effect upon it. Others are essential to the life of the garden, maintaining the precious balance. And there are those that forever bring change. The hope, always, is that some new, wonderful strain of rose appears.

I'm most fond of these English gardens, woven to seem so unpretentious. But I am all too aware of the love and care that go into their growth, and the pride that comes in the moments spent reflecting on their splendor.

# MORNING PAPERS

I was ten years old when I started my paper route. I'd wake at 5:30, fold thirty copies of *The Halifax Herald* and be off as fast as my feet could carry me. Some of my customers wanted their papers left in a particular place. I was only happy to oblige, since as a businessman my motto was "Keep the customer." However, once I'd saved up enough to buy a bike, the news now and then became something the customer had to look up to (landing on the roof) or look around for (like under a big, tall, long-armed evergreen). Spot, my faithful dog, was with me every day. He was an independent partner every so often along the way, but we always came home together.

There was so much to see that I really enjoyed my route. The morning air was crisp and clear as the sunshine lit up the homes and gardens where I grew up. When I had the chance, I'd pick up a stick as I ran alongside a picket fence. The sound was music to my ears, and the faster I ran, the better the music. I loved the roads I took each day, as well as the change of seasons. Birds sang as I looked at the old boats and boathouses in the harbor. Some were brightened up by daffodils and crocus and other early risers of spring. As for summer, I loved a morning swim after my deliveries. In the fall, leaves in their bright autumn colors crunched under my feet. During freezing winters I braved the deep snow. Great, big, white clouds of steam rose from the trains as I stopped and watched them from the bridge over the tracks.

One of my brothers had a route with fifty customers, and I always hoped to finish mine before he finished his. Lots of his customers were in apartment buildings, though, so I never did. I think I saw much more on my route anyway, and in that

*The Paperboy*
(Above) *You can see lots of things when you are a paperboy, and at that time in the morning, the neighborhood was yours. While everyone was still behind closed doors, the spacious streets gave way to the ever-changing patterns the huge, old trees cast on green grass and white fences on bright, sunny days.*

*Morning Papers*
(Detail) I remember
the clickety-clack of the
stick as I ran it along the
fence. It was a joy to my
ears back then. I wonder
if the sleeping neighbors
felt the same.

[57]

### Sunday Afternoon
*A quiet afternoon to share a dream or two.*

### Schoolboys
*(Previous pages) Autumn chores await these two before the serious fun can begin. Of course, Old Faithful will be with them, ready to do whatever they want.*

respect I finished way ahead of him. I delivered my papers until I was thirteen. The route took an hour until I got my bike; then it took only forty-five minutes. As soon as we got home, we would have breakfast and walk the mile and a half to school by 8:00. For most kids the day had just begun, but I always felt like I'd seen a big part of the world by then.

Even though I delivered the papers Monday through Saturday, the best day was Saturday. I collected the weekly fee from each customer by noon, and sometimes they would say, "Keep the change." If all my keeps added up to twenty-five cents, I would race to the Welcome Cafe where Mr. Chin made the best butterscotch pie in the world. It was served with a big glass of ice-cold milk. I was as happy as could be.

P.S.—Butterscotch pie is still my favorite.

### Verandah
*Though the peacefulness and a quiet book deserve savoring on this summer day, the*

occasional stirring of the bay winds calls for a glance at the view
every now and then. The place on the page may be lost, but the
moments of reverie are just as enjoyable—perhaps even more so.

### Apple Blossom Time
*Spring, the season of rebirth, calls for celebrating the fragrance, the splash of delicate color, the sunshine—as well as the spending of time with each other outdoors on an afternoon picnic.*

## THE GREAT CART ADVENTURE

My older brother, Joe, and I were out in the barn, looking for something to invent. With our large family, we had to get creative in order to entertain ourselves. I spied an old wooden crate up in the rafters. Just like that, I knew what we were going to do—we were going to make the best cart the world had ever seen.

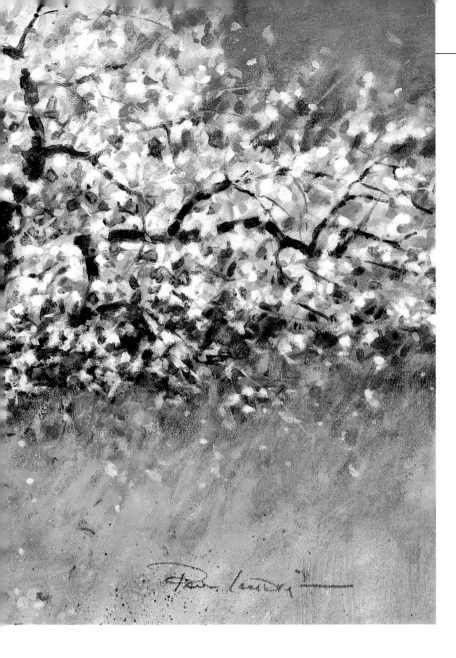

Looking down the hill, we spotted a problem. The wheels on the cart were attached firmly in place, and at the bottom the road made a sharp right turn. We had no way to steer the thing! Joe suggested that we jump out of the cart once the road started to curve. It wasn't the best of plans, because we could only use the cart once. After we jumped, it would sail out over a rocky cliff and down into the bay. I came up with leaning to one side, using the weight of our bodies to shift the cart's course and follow the road. We decided that we would try this method.

Joe was about to take off on the cart's maiden voyage when our tagalong younger brother John showed up. We told him to go away, but he wouldn't. We told him he wasn't old enough to ride in the cart, so he sat on the grass and watched us. Joe folded himself into the cart and took off down the hill. Boy, did that cart go! I started screaming at Joe to tilt to the right. He did, and the cart followed the road to the right. It actually worked!

Now it was my turn. Squeezing myself into the cart, I found that there was no way that jumping out before the cart went over the edge would ever work. I said a little prayer as Joe gave the cart a good push. What a ride! It seemed like I was going 100 miles an hour. Trees and bushes were screaming past as I got closer and closer to the cliff. I shifted my weight and closed my eyes. All I could hear was the sound of the pebbles from the road under the wheels, not the silence of flying through the air. I opened my eyes—I had made the corner. I told Joe about the great ride I had, but I didn't let him know I had shut my eyes.

A half-hour later, we were bored with the cart. We were climbing a huge rock nearby when we heard the sound of the cart rolling down the hill. It was John. He had waited until we left and must have decided it was his turn. By

I climbed into the rafters of the barn and tossed the crate down to my brother. It was a good, sturdy crate and would hold our weight without falling to pieces. Joe went off in search of wheels, and I looked for a hammer and nails. Joe came back with four wheels that looked a lot like they belonged to our baby sister's carriage. For a split second, I wondered how long it would be until my mother would want to take her for a ride. We attached them to the crate, added a pull rope and we were ready to go.

We took the cart to the top of the hill near the bay.

## Cape Cod Window

*(Above) Just imagine sitting on the other side of this window, and enjoying some lobster stew in this cottage with an ocean view.*

## Southport

*Southport is an admirable spot year-round. Like many of Connecticut's centuries-old shoreline communities, it's filled with wonderful homes, fences, gardens and lanes just waiting to be explored.*

the time we saw him, John was at the curve in the road. We screamed at the top of our lungs, "Tilt, John, tilt!" He didn't hear us. Moments later John went sailing out over the cliff.

We raced down to the bottom of the cliff where John lay bleeding. We were sure he was dead. We just didn't know what to do. There was silence except for the sound of the water. Then John made a little mewling sound. He was still alive! Thank

God the cart wasn't broken because we used it to carry John, twisted and bloody, back to the farmhouse.

Fittingly, the sky was getting dark with clouds as we approached the farm. We placed him on the back steps of the house, knocked on the door and ran like hell. As we hid behind a huge bush, our mother carefully brought him inside. Joe and I just sat there, too scared to go in. Moments later she was out on the porch, screaming our names. The jig was up. We were really going to get it this time.

Inside, my father, a doctor, had just finished looking over John's injuries and told us that he was going to be fine. The two of us would be responsible for his chores until he was able to do them again. No reproaches, and no questions, but after dinner Mum mentioned that the wheels were missing from the baby carriage. The next day, doing John's chores around the barn, I noticed another crate up in the rafters, larger and sturdier than the first. Yes, this would definitely make the best cart ever.

## Sunflowers

(Left) Among artists, Rockport, Massachusetts, is perhaps the most popular of New England's coastal towns. It may be over-painted, but how could I resist this view from the garden?

## Seaport Garden, Mystic

I enjoy visiting Mystic. There is always something new and interesting to see in this old place. The gardens are well tended, and the river speaks for itself.

# MY GARDEN

I garden for the love of it. It helps me stay aware of things that really matter—the simple, natural things in life. I think gardeners have a strong appreciation for life, the outdoors and faith, and I believe that if everyone could garden, it would be a better world. Now I understand why Mum and Dad loved to garden, and I hope that I also pass this tradition on to my children. Except for the time I went to school in New York City, I don't believe that I have ever lived in a home without at least a small garden. I can't wait to get up in the morning, or to come home from a trip, to see what's happening to the growing things—after, of course, I greet my wife, Mary, and the children.

Gardening has been a family tradition. My painting *The Captain's Garden* is my interpretation of my grandfather's garden in Cape Breton. I never met him—he died many years before I was born—but I like to think that this was the way it

*Summer Delight*

*Sunshine and Flowers*
(Far left) A day for Hope and dreams among the sunstruck flowers and gentle fragrances.

was with Cecilia, his wife, and one of their thirteen children—possibly even my father's twin, Lillian, walking with Cecilia. The garden would just have to have been there: It was where my father learned to love gardening so much.

On our farm in St. Margaret's Bay, he would spend hours working the soil. He especially loved his vegetable garden on the hillside. Often, the chore of the day was hilling the potatoes. We had row after row; it was a huge garden and it took forever. The task wasn't all that pleasurable at the time, but is very memorable now.

My mother loved her flowers. She had her flower patches all about the house. We'd see her out there, day after day, in her broad sun hat. She had a very special knack for her flowers. I believe that she conversed with them and they with her. Judging from the results, it must have been a mutual relationship of love and praise. As she grew older, she still tended her gardens, and won awards for her prized roses right through her eighties.

The gardening heritage in New England is no different from that of Nova Scotia. The earliest gardeners were everyday, hearty people with a small plot of land and a family to feed. The season was short and the land rugged, but being strong-willed stock, they succeeded. As these vegetable gardens developed, flowers were introduced, planted from the seeds of wildflowers that grew around their cottage doors. The flowers were used for color and fragrance. Herbs, of course, were a health and cooking necessity, their seeds and use going back generations.

I suppose the gardens to which I am most attracted are English cottage gardens. They are

*Summer Arbor*
*Hollyhocks offer a standing welcome as they show off their dazzling charm.*

*Splish Splash*
*(Above) Garden visitors
keep cool.*

*Matthew's Bench*
*(Left) The early light of a
new day on its way through
my garden finds even this hand-
made bench teeming with life.*

generally free-growing, not stiff or laid out, or at least they give a delightfully informal appearance. The plants, tall or short, and of whatever color, jumble together, looking as though nature intended them to grow thick and close, covering the ground entirely in great masses of color and texture. But oh, how their owners tend and love those natural-looking gardens. And like the English custom, folks in New England share their joy with neighbors and friends, along with slips and cuttings passed over the fence. True cottage gardeners.

My own garden is an extension of my studio. I have a variety of trellises and arbors that I've made. Patio containers and window boxes adorn the house as well. To bring even more life into the garden, there are birdhouses and birdbaths. A path is important as a design element as much as it is for strolling among the flowers. I have benches to rest on, and a quiet place for an afternoon cup of tea.

Finally, the white picket fence: It would not be New England without one. It's really not to keep anything out, but rather to enhance and protect the flowers in front and in back of it—a frame, as it were. The contrast between the white of the fence and the dark of the greens is what I enjoy most about them. I've found that I really need a garden in my life: the color, textures and abundant fragrances stimulate my heart and soul.

*Four O'Clock Tea*
*(Left) Tea on the verandah near the sea, where both fragrances mix into a special blend all their own.*

*Del's Tea Rose*
*George's gift.*

## Hollyhocks
(Above) *Bright and beautiful,*
*these are a favorite in many a*
*New Englander's garden.*

# GARDENING'S OTHER SIDE

Even the gentlest of gardeners can become enraged when confronted with insects and other marauders. Raymond, the boatbuilder, had a large, fenced-in vegetable garden back behind his barns, right at the edge of the woods. One morning we saw the local game warden arriving at Raymond's house. They both headed off to the garden. Knowing Raymond, we figured that something was up. We took a short cut across the hay fields and caught up with them as they arrived at the problem. Right there in the fenced-in garden was the biggest buck moose I had ever seen. The rack on his head could have held thirty hats, easy.

Raymond was complaining to the game warden with a rather strong note of protest: "The blankety-blank's eating my garden! My family will starve this winter! I've got the right to shoot the blankety-blank thing right now!" No, he did not, the warden pronounced. Not until hunting season. However, if the moose did not get out over the next couple of days, he would reconsider.

So, of course, Raymond made sure that the moose stayed in the garden. The next day, the moose was still there. Bright and early the day after that, the warden drove up. He was followed by half a dozen cars and trucks filled with curious folks from the village. Word always got around fast where Raymond was concerned.

We joined the crowd that was headed for the garden. Sure enough, there in the middle, enjoying Raymond's turnips, was the moose. He was truly a gigantic, huge, grandfather-of-them-all moose. He looked up once at the crowd, then chose to ignore us and continue feeding. We all tried to scare him by jumping up and down and yelling. A few sticks were thrown, but he went right on placidly feeding. He had now reached the cabbages. That, even to the game warden, seemed to be the last straw. He decided to let Raymond have his way, and Raymond headed back to his house to get his rifle.

Now the crowd started to have mixed emotions. Most there were farmers, and well used to the need to slaughter animals. But this was different. The moose was fenced in, and it didn't seem like he could get out. No one could even tell how he got in there to begin with. Raymond arrived back with his gun about the same time as one of my brothers with our fox terrier, Spot. Instantly, the real drama began.

Spot spied the moose and was off across the garden like a flash. The moose noticed this little beast coming at him like David against Goliath. Ponderously, the great beast turned and headed for the far fence, gathering speed as he went. Spot was able to catch up and actually nip at his great hooves. With this, the moose gathered himself up and took a tremendous leap, his thousands of pounds soaring right over the fence. You don't get to see a flying moose every day; moreover, it happened so fast that we were all stunned.

Spot had saved the moose. Raymond was totally shocked. As we walked away from the farm, proud and happy of the great job Spot had done, Raymond had begun to speak his own mind on the matter: "Blankety-blank-blank-blank . . ."

*Afternoon Tea*
(Detail, right) A pristine location for the enjoyment of sunny afternoons and a cup of tea.

*Cottage Garden*
(Below) A garden where something is always in bloom.

# Countryside Markets

All the freshly picked vegetables would be ready and waiting in their bins.

# *Countryside Markets*

*Aunt Martha's Country Farm (Detail)* One of the nice things about being an artist is having the opportunity to capture moments and memories that are significant to you and then pass them on to others. This countryside cornucopia was an actual place, as was Aunt Martha a real person. Having been there, I can tell you that it's a place you'd love to go to right now.

The country is important to me, not only for the generous gift of the colorful palette, the endless variety of textures and the ever-present fragrances, but for the fact that it is a real joy to the heart. All growing things, but especially flowers, have been a big part of my life. I envy people that can remember the picturesque names, but as for me, I know that flowers evoke memories. It's their nature.

As kids, we all had to work both in my mum's flower garden and in my dad's vegetable plot. Gardening then seemed like a tedious chore, but without really becoming aware of it, I must have grown to know and love flowers. I like to think that my work conveys this.

Art and artists are often the subject of great scrutiny. There are many things that an artist has to fall back on: technical proficiency and the work ethic that got him or her there, subject and even, sometimes, a really good frame. But at the core of this are the artist and the honesty with which the artist approaches art. This is true for painters, writers, sculptors, teachers, farmers or fishermen.

It isn't necessary that artists "live the life" that they have chosen to depict. But those who do, or have that intimate knowledge and relationship with their subject, can't help but to have that show through. Even before I stretch the canvas or dip my brush in paint, I search my heart for those things that are the most powerful reminders of remembered times and places.

## THE FLOWER MARKET

One of the really wonderful things about life in the country is wandering the back roads and byways. A stranger from out of town doing so might have been lucky to happen upon Aunt Martha's, but locally Aunt Martha's was famous. If you didn't grow something in your own garden, or even if you did, the lure of this roadside farm was irresistible. It gave the impression that this was the way it was supposed to be. Aunt Martha was simply as you would imagine her to be, and she made that experience complete.

It was fine to stop by at any time, but to be there on a brand-new morning was glorious. Aunt Martha was always there with the sun, as the early day's warm, bright light reflected off the dew-covered, sweet-scented flowers. Nothing can beat that smell of fresh, damp green. The morning's long shadows would stretch lazily along the well-worn path leading in. All the freshly picked vegetables would be ready and glistening in their bins: delicious varieties of peppers, squash and huge, ripe tomatoes.

*Summer Potpourri*
*(Above, left) Changing patterns of light and shade dance around this rainbow of color.*

## Flower Market

Another summer day has arrived, and the flower market, like a gracious hostess, is ready with an abundant mixture of sweet fragrances and the entire tantalizing spectrum of color, to welcome you with her arms open wide.

## Flowers for Mary Hope

(Left) My Mary is carefully choosing just the right assortment of flowers to give to our daughter. Our daughter's full name is Mary Hope, but we call her Hope. I thought that the title "Flowers for Hope" would be too misleading, so I used her full name.

## Mary Hope

The recipient of the flowers, my delightful daughter. Today, Hope is an actress with an angelic voice. She still loves flowers, especially on opening night.

Every once in a while, special invitations would be issued for friends and neighbors to stop by, but anyone who happened to be passing was welcome. They would be greeted by a smiling Aunt Martha. She always had time to chat, whether she was waiting on someone, refilling the bins or making sure that the flowers didn't get too thirsty. Not only was she an exquisite gardener, but she was a great cook, too. Usually she had a linen-lined basket loaded with huge, fruit-filled muffins to share—warm, scrumptious and light as air. They were just as luscious as her homemade breads and strawberry or peach jams.

Aunt Martha's roadside farm market was the gardener's equivalent of the main-street barber shop: the informal meeting place of plant lovers in our town. Even if you weren't buying something, you could have a joyful time swapping hints and stories. No doubt the ladies got into recipes as well. There should be an Aunt Martha's in everybody's life.

## Petunias

*I'd like to meet the person who came up with the idea of flower boxes. I have yet to encounter a home that didn't benefit from their lively, beautiful presence.*

**Little Flower Shop**
(Center) *Pretty as a picture. When I came across this shop, it wasn't long before it became one.*

**Flower Shop**
*A splash of color, not to go unnoticed, emerges again and again as the shadows crisscross the alleyway.*

*A Floral Rainbow*
*Reflections in the morning*
*mist lead to the pot of gold*
*at the end of the rainbow.*

# HORSE AND WAGON

A horse and wagon was a common sight when I was a boy. Daily they'd come trundling by bringing fruit, vegetables, ice, milk and eggs to the homes in the neighborhood. Everyone knew the drivers, and each driver knew his customers and what a particular family might need. Basically, the drivers and the families were friends.

I remember the Taylors. Mr. Taylor used to load up his wagon with freshly gathered vegetables and deliver them in our locality. While he

was out doing his job, his kids and I would use the big, old crates from his barn to make really great forts. We had a marvelous time as our imaginations ran wild. We'd be soldiers protecting our territory from who knows what deadly enemy, or besieged heroes behind the towering battlements. Whatever was attacking us, we knew that our magnificent forts would protect us.

Mr. Taylor never yelled at us for messing up his crates, although there were times when he would scowl at us ferociously. He was really very good at that. I believe that we all felt we had been successful at our day when he pulled a particularly mad face.

*Flower Wagon*
*The flower man was a friend to all. The pleasure he brought to his customers remained long after his wagon was gone.*

### The Flower Barn
*(Previous pages) Warm sunlight and fresh flowers for sale called my attention to this old country facade.*

### Christmas at the Flower Market
*Once again, that special spirit of Christmas fills the air and, in this case, the flower market as*

*well. The patchwork fields of color that blessed this place in summer have been replaced by the verdant greens and reds of winter.*

*The Antique Shop*
*Treasured are those moments when we see an old friend from childhood days.*

Milkmen were another group who were still big users of the horse and wagon, and my friend Irving's father was one. Now he had the neatest horse. When Irving's father left the wagon to carry bottles of milk to his customers, his horse would plod on past two or three houses and then come to a stop. Following the horse, along would come Irving's father, ready to serve more customers along their route. How his horse knew exactly where to go and when to stop amazed me. Not only that, it really seemed like he was leading Irving's father. That was just one smart horse, I guess.

# UPON THE BONNY SHORES OF ENGLAND

Tradition and heritage have always meant a lot in my family. I grew up in Canada and now live in America—New England, actually. The Maritimes, as they are known a little farther north, share with this part of the United States their roots: England. Though I no longer live where I grew up, the core of that place is still with me. In the same way, colonists on the eastern seaboard brought with them bits and pieces as well. The country cottage became the Cape Cod cottage; gardens grew, but with new varieties. They even brought the names of their villages with them.

The opportunity to go to England came up, and I had never been there before. Where to start? I wanted both to see what interested me visually, and to know its history. I went to the library for reference, reading and getting ideas on villages, cottages, gardens and seashore. The first thing I found I could eliminate were the cities. With further examination of the maps, it seemed to me that the rural areas were not all that extensive and that these could be divided into three sections: the middle and the two ends.

The first trip was to the Cotswolds and its quaint villages. This is the land of Shakespeare's Stratford-upon-Avon, and the famous cottage of Anne Hathaway, his wife. Her cottage was three stories high, and about one-third of it was used as a barn. Somewhat different than I had expected. I stayed at the White Lion in Upton-upon-Severn, not only one of the main locations of the novel *Tom Jones*, but where it was written as well.

The next two trips were to the fishing villages and towns of Cornwall and Devon. Fishing communities around the world may, on the surface, seem quite different. However,

## English Market

(Below) The village market in England is a place where the atmosphere is friendly as shoppers browse from stall to stall.

## English Pub

No English village would be complete without a pub or two. I am familiar with this one in the village of Upton because I have been there many times to enjoy the pub grub accompanied by a pint or two.

### Morning Walk
Stepping out onto the river bank  these brave little fellows
follow their confident leader for a waddle in the sunshine.

### Girl Reading
(Below) A quiet spot to sit and relax.

*Garden Door*
*(Detail) Many an English cottage
has a special entry to some vibrant
little cultivated patch. The love of
gardening is obvious here.*

if you've grown up in one, the sights, sounds, smells and even the people are strikingly familiar. It was absolutely beautiful.

The crown jewel of my trips to England was the time spent in the Lake District. The country is lyrically beautiful, the villages neat and the people friendly. Writers and artists have a passionate affection for this region. Annually, it attracts thousands, and now I understand why.

I was especially taken with the area around Lake Windermere, and with Beatrix Potter's country farm. Beatrix was a storyteller and artist for all ages, who passed away nearly fifty years ago. She was best known for creating Peter Rabbit. Walking through the villages of Hawkshead and Sawrey, the settings for some of her tales, was fascinating, like walking on sacred ground.

I went on to Hilltop Farm, and up a path with gardens on both sides. It leads to the farmhouse she used for a studio, in which she wrote and illustrated her beloved stories. To think that the Puddle-ducks took that same path or Peter Rabbit once bounded by!

Born in London, Beatrix Potter vacationed in the Lake District as a young girl. She fell in love with the area, incorporated it in her writing and soon bought Hilltop Farm with the royalties she earned on her early books. This was the start of her deep interest in farming and her life-long, loving concern for the Lake District. She would eventually buy up fifteen farms in the region and rent them out to tenants. Early on, she had perceived the threat to the landscape and realized that only through ownership and control of the essential assets of the Lake District's farming life could it be safeguarded. Her four thousand acres of land, farmhouse and cottages were left to the National Trust.

This lady was as interesting as the characters she wrote about. There's a story told about her always wearing a bonnet in her garden: they say that sometimes the bonnet was replaced by a large rhubarb leaf. She must have had a keen sense of humor, one just as deep and sincere as her love for the subjects of her stories and paintings. As with any artist, it shows through.

*An English Cottage*
*This cottage, bathed in sunshine, caught my eye and I couldn't pass it by. Could that be Anne Hathaway feeding the chickens?*

### Beatrix Potter's Hilltop Farm

When visiting England's Lake District and Hilltop Farm, I felt like I was in a place of worship. It's a congregation dedicated to the land where Beatrix Potter was the first and most devoted follower. Her love of flowers and animals is an inspiration to me.

**Cottage Reflections and Front Garden**
*(Top right; bottom right) The rewards of
tender, loving care.*

# Picket Fences

*Some homes come
with tradition
built in; all you
have to do is
turn the key.*

# Picket Fences

A home is the combination of many things: structure, people, time and, most of all, love. It's the whole of these parts that makes up one of the most consistent aspects of our lives. It's easy to think that simply buying or renting a house or apartment technically makes a home. You can add in all of your possessions and change things to make the place uniquely yours, but only through the accumulation of care, experience and time does the house you are living in become a home.

That is not to say that certain homes don't come with a great deal of history, charm and personality already built in. Imagine the feeling of moving into the White House (albeit with only a four-year guarantee), a castle above some misty loch or the House of Seven Gables. The houses of New England come with tradition, and all you have to do is simply turn the key.

Neighbors and communities have as much influence upon a home as what happens under its roof. In St. Margaret's Bay, the man next door was responsible for half the fun of living there. Our one-room schoolhouse kept all the kids from town in constant touch. I consider these people and experiences as much a part of any home I've ever had.

The houses that I have lived in have always had certain things in common. Some of those were sought out; others were either built or grown, and some, well, they just came with the territory. But always it has been the passage of time that has made it a home.

# HUMBLE, SIMPLE AND BEAUTIFUL

The dictionary defines "cottage" as a small house. I think that this description could be expanded, especially for my favorite, the Cape Cod cottage. The "Cape" is distinctly American, despite its English origin. It traces back to Devon and Cornwall on the south coast of England. In this country, they like to say that the Cape Cod style of cottage is homegrown and evolved in Plymouth, Massachusetts.

The fact is, the Pilgrims, simple and logical people, built their homes like the ones they had left behind in England. It was what they knew, and besides, the style had the distinct advantage of being easy to build. They were accustomed to small, rectangular, one-story homes with steep gable roofs,

## Rose Hill
*(Left) Roses adorning both sides of this hill greet a sailor returning home from the sea and make this a delightful lane to travel.*

## Rambling Rose
*(Opposite) The arrival of warm air over cool water meant fog. The great trellis of climbing roses brightens this cottage by the bay in spite of the fog.*

## Floral Cottage
*Nestled in colorful flowers is this joyful little hideaway at the end of a small road near the sea.*

### Nantucket Lane

*These little seaside homes are surrounded by all kinds of flowers and hugged close by picket fences.*

which, of course at that time, would have been thatch-covered.

The early cottage consisted of one room, with a fireplace used for both heating and cooking. A ladder led to an open loft for sleeping and the storage of food. A fire burned constantly in the fireplace. Even though there was a chimney, the single room must have been dark and musty.

Many of the older Cape Cod cottages we see today were built by the seafaring men of New England: the carpenters, shipwrights and fishermen. Their homes were constructed like their ships and boats—sturdy, practical and set low to withstand the winds borne by the sea. Living in Capes has been a big part of my life.

My favorites (and how I like to paint them) are those set back off the road. They do not dominate the land about them, like a mansion. More, they are part of their space, nestled snugly in their surroundings of trees and gardens. A favorite element is the white picket fence, centered with a trellis of roses to invite visitors in. The distinct, broad roof with a plump, white chimney is the icing on the cake of these quaint gems. Humble, simple and beautiful, these cottages are uniquely our own.

*A Winding Country Road*
*Sharing the time of day on the lane, just up from the waterside.*

# THE HANDYMAN

Thoughts of household repairs always lead me to Raymond. Nothing much, except to replace a few shingles here and there, had been done to our roof since the hurricane that had made it possible for my dad to buy our property in St. Margaret's Bay. We had been living at the farm for quite a while when the time came to put on a new roof. It happened to be a slow time for fishermen, so our multitalented neighbor (and foe of our dog, Spot) was hired to do the job.

My brothers and I were totally impressionable, and Raymond was a very impressive fellow. It seemed that there was nothing he couldn't do. Exceedingly curious, we climbed up to watch, hoping to learn how to reshingle. Raymond didn't really seem all that busy, moving slowly over the roof. But every now and then, he'd hammer one of his fingers. Immediately, we'd hear a blast of the salty language that Raymond spoke so naturally and so well.

We found this vastly amusing because the only bad word we knew was "arse." His words might have embarrassed the most hardened of men for all we knew, because we had no idea what he was saying, really. We simply loved the sound and volume of what we were sure were terrible swear words—and, of course, the look on his face.

*Cape Cod Cottage*
(Detail) I'm strongly attracted to the charm of Cape Cod cottages, a distinct New England tradition with roots back in the villages of England.

*Harbor Hill*
(Overleaf) A wide road to the harbor is bordered by big, old homes with their glorious flowers. It's an open road for all to enjoy, at any time.

*Flower Baskets*
(Upper right) Climbing baskets border the window's edge.

*Cape Cod Welcome*
(Right) The rose-scented doorway adds to the welcome
you'll find here.

## Cottage Path

(Far left) A Cape cottage defines New England and Americana for me. I like the simple design of the cottage, and when there are flowers around it, well, that's perfect for me.

## Arbor Roses

Trellises adorned with flowers make for lots of color at every bend of the garden path.

We couldn't wait for another slip of the hammer. It should be noted, though, that he never used his salty talk when a female was within hearing.

Raymond liked to tease us with far-fetched claims. He said that if he felt like it, he could shingle our roof with a hammer in each hand while holding the nails between his toes. Or his teeth. He said that he was the fastest nailer in the bay. Knowing Raymond, I'd say he probably was—just a mite bit fanciful about his methods.

Raymond's brother once put him to the test. There was a massive stack of firewood that needed to be split and corded for the coming winter season. His wife and brother were pressing him to get on with the job, as winter was com-

### Side by Side
*(Left) Twin windows are surrounded by a charming climbing rose.*

### Fisherman's Cottage
*A love-filled cottage along the way.*

ing soon. Raymond said, "It's no blankety-blank problem. I'll cut and split the blankety-blank wood in two blankety-blank days."

Raymond's brother bet him a case of Moosehead that he couldn't do it in two weeks, much less two days. He never should have made a bet with Raymond. Working straight through the day and under lamplight at night, Raymond got the entire job done in two days. He piled the wood so high it hid the chicken coop. From that time on, nobody doubted the will of the Paul Bunyan of the Bay.

But back to the roof. My brother decided to set up the fastest roofer we knew with a problem we had from school: he asked him to decline a sentence. (Declension was the current lesson that our teacher,

Raymond's wife, was giving.) The sentence was "The white seagull flew over the roof." Raymond paused in his nailing and gave a serious, contemplative look. My brother and I were all smiles, thinking that we had "got" him. He went back to his shingling and, without missing a beat, studiously announced, " The white blankety-blank seagull flew over the blankety-blank roof and blankety-blanked on the other side." We almost fell off the roof laughing.

We didn't dare repeat Raymond's sayings, and indeed, I doubt that we could have reproduced the remarkable fluency of his language. We learned a lot more than how to hammer in a shingle in Raymond's roofing lessons, and the other kids in school didn't know what they were missing.

## Gramp's Shaving Mug
*(Above) My mother's father, Angus Morrison, used to use this mug.*

## Flower Boxes
*This home is in an old shipbuilding town in Connecticut. Many of the homes there have signs indicating their building dates and the owners' names and occupations.*

## Victorian Memories
(Right) Cape May, another
historical community, is
a Victorian delight: one
old gingerbread home
followed by another.

## Summer Daisies
Some of Uncle Tom's daisies
rest on our baby's afghan.

*Daydreamer,*
*Martha's*
*Vineyard*
*Martha's Vineyard*
*is a delightful place*
*to visit. When I*
*came upon this*
*house, I could just*
*picture Bimmer*
*sitting on our old*
*rocking chair in*
*this cozy corner.*
*So that's where*
*I put him.*

# Hometown Celebrations

I think that
every day is a cause
for a celebration:
a celebration
of life.

# Hometown Celebrations

**Spring Song**
*The church and dogwoods are from the town where I live in Connecticut. The wedding is of the period I feel is most romantic. I hope that this song of hope, love, trust and joy fills their hearts with happiness forever.*

On one of my research trips, I took a tour of some old homes. Even though it was August at the time, the thought of Christmas came to mind when I saw a room with a flight of steps tucked in near the fireplace and leading up to a door next to a window. I could just picture the big tree dominating the room, with decorations on the windows, door and banister; stockings hung by the fireplace; candles lit and assorted toys near the tree. From personal experience, I knew that the parents had been up late on Christmas Eve, while the children had hardly slept a wink in anticipation of opening the surprises Santa had left behind.

Christmas, perhaps the most obvious of our celebrations, is the one that we put the most energy into. The thoughts, feelings and emotions that come with, and that we attach to, that event are not things that should be put away in a closet and not used again until next year. I do my best to keep those perceptions with me at all times.

Throughout the year, we are presented with national holidays to which we are supposed to apply certain emotions. It's hard to grasp these, sometimes, on a national scale, much less a global one. I prefer to let these celebrations take on the feeling of how I experience them in my own home and town. They are much more personal that way. To become aware of the things that build up to and follow these events is just as special. Then those emotions and feelings are spread beyond any one particular day. Capturing this is central to my work.

# CELEBRATIONS

I think that every day is a celebration: a celebration of life. It's what you put into it, and what you take out. Celebrations come in all shapes and sizes, some created and some given. It could be as simple as a quiet stroll along the seashore with someone special: a personal, private time to remember. It might be as important as a spring wedding: the celebration of two hearts joined as one, where even the sunshine and blooming flowers seem to give their blessings to the bride and groom.

For some folks, it might be the first concert of the summer season, and knowing that you have a standing invitation for those to come. And what about a child's first carousel ride? Music fills the air, and there are all those ponies to choose from. The ride begins, and as the wind brushes upon that young face, a great, big smile from the heart appears. Only by catching the brass ring could that be made better.

A favorite standard is the hometown parade. I love them. With parades, it doesn't matter whether you're in it or not. You become part of them as you wave, cheer, clap your hands or tap your toes to the marching bands that go by. It's important that we have the tradition of honoring all those heroes who were and are so brave. Just seeing the faces and their uniforms makes my heart swell with pride. And the summer picnic that follows simply keeps the celebration going all that much longer.

*Summer Concert*
*(Diptych) These days must have been wonderful: the music of the band, the decorated gazebo, the sunshine, the townsfolk, the horses and carriages, benches to relax on and the whole happy*

atmosphere. I am still able to capture some of this in my own personal life. My son Tom (the boy with the hoop) modeled for me. Today he himself has grown into a fine musician, and I enjoy his concerts, too.

### Hometown Parade

I love parades, anytime, anywhere. The spirit is contagious as the soldiers march by with Old Glory, leading the way. The bands play as they strut tall and proud. Children not watching from a father's shoulders run alongside in a formation all their own. Balloons float

*above the crowd gathered at the roadside, occasionally breaking free for destinations unknown. Everyone is full of pride to be in the land of the free and the home of the brave.*

There is, of course, fresh air, sunshine and some time to relax. For some folks, a Sunday afternoon's pleasure was a trip to the boardwalk. In between the blue water and the little shops, where you could get a hot dog and a lemonade, a frozen custard, a souvenir or some saltwater taffy, was the actual boardwalk. Here people could stroll arm in arm, take a ride in a pushcart or on a bicycle—all to the sounds of the boardwalk music hall. For the daring, there were the hold-tight thrills of the roller coaster. It was the county fair that never went away.

Parks were and are always the place to go to enjoy some quiet time, either walking or just sitting on a bench. All around you, the wonders of nature are so generously shared. They are also a good place to be when autumn comes around and nature displays her finest fall wardrobe. The country markets become a festival of rainbows: mums to brighten up baskets inside and out; apples, cold, crisp and delicious, just waiting to become pies, sauce and dumplings; tasty squash and pumpkins for carving and for soups and bread. The whole of fall is a celebration of the joyous brilliance of color and light.

Then, shortly after October, the first snowfall arrives. This, perhaps, is the greatest unofficial holiday on any child's roster. Out came the sleds and shovels. The rivers froze; ice hockey and crack the whip were the order of the day. Snow forts were built, and walks among the glistening trees in snow-covered woods produced the perfect cone-shaped candidate for Christmas morning.

At some point, even as we enjoy the days of winter, a single crocus pokes its head up through the snow. Soon other buds start to appear, then blossom till spring fills our heads and hearts all over again.

### A Place in the Park
*I think that a park is a great place, and I always enjoy park settings. There's no end to the impressions they make on my heart.*

Every day gives me reason to celebrate; every day provides cause for thanksgiving for all of the blessings in my life: my family, friends, and career. God knows how much I'm thankful for the talents He's given me, and for the beautiful life I live. The love that surrounds me and the encouragement I receive humble me. Yes, every day is a reason to celebrate.

*Boardwalk Promenade*
*Enjoying the boardwalk was the thing to do for both the young and old, alone or not—a time to relax, a time for yourself. You might savor a piece of saltwater taffy*

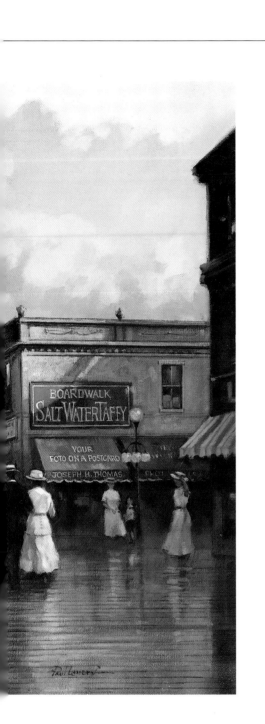

or a frozen custard. Now and then you could hear the distant music of the concert hall as you strolled along, just happy to be alive.

### Children's Carousel
*What a ride it was! And remember, the best part of all was when you asked if you could have another ride and you heard, "Okay, but just one more."*

### Sail Watchers
*It was always a pleasure to watch the sails go by as we chatted with our friends on a Sunday afternoon.*

**Summer Regatta**
*Before its arrival in England, and eventually America, the term "regatta" came from the gondola races in Venice.*

## A DOG CALLED SPOT

It's not an easy thing to gift wrap a dog. However, my father had brought home a fox terrier, and I decided that this would make the greatest birthday present for my older brother, Joe. I wrapped the dog in some paper and cut four holes for his legs. You should have seen the faces on my family when this package literally walked into the room! Joe was crazy about the dog and named him after the spotted markings on his body.

Sometimes Spot would let Joe and me follow him on

his adventures, but generally he was more of a free spirit. He would disappear for hours without a trace, coming and going as he chose. It happened that one of our neighbors had a farm where he kept cows, hens and other animals. Once Spot discovered the henhouse, the trouble started. He'd bark like crazy and send the hens into a frenzy. They'd start flying in the air, cackling madly, crashing into one another in mid-flight and falling to the floor, practically unconscious.

Our neighbor came to call on my father and talk over the problems he was having in his henhouse. He had seen Spot coming and going from his farm quite a bit, and assumed it was he who was disturbing the birds. My father had no choice but to agree and assured him that the problem would be remedied. Something had to be done about Spot, and since we were all opposed to confining or chaining him, we'd have to give him away.

That summer our cat, Twinkle, had a litter of five kittens. Whenever she sensed danger, Twinkle would take the kittens from the box on the back porch, which served as their home, and hide them. About the time that the neighbor came to talk with my father about Spot, Twinkle hid all five of her kittens.

For two panicked days, we searched for the kittens. We looked in all the usual hiding places, but no luck. As I was off one day to do my chores, I went by the box and

*Regatta Time*
*The flags danced in the sunshine, and excitement filled the air on this special regatta day. It was always an elegant and respected social function.*

found that, suddenly, three of the kittens were back. Up in the apple orchard I came across Spot. In his mouth he held another of the kittens, and the last one he was trying to push along in front of him. It kept him quite busy because only the one in his mouth was willing to keep still. Now all the kittens had finally been brought home, and we had none other than Spot to thank for it. My father had a change of heart, and agreed to let us keep him.

Some time later, Spot ran away (maybe). My mother told us he had probably run off with a sailor, who would take Spot out to sea on his journeys. We didn't know whether to believe this story or not, but, knowing Spot, it just could be. So in our imaginations, then and forever, Spot continues to live a life of wild adventure—the only kind he really liked.

### Seaside Carousel
*(Above) The music was wonderful. Your hands gripped the brass pole; the cool breeze was on your face, and round and round you'd go, wishing it would never stop.*

### Autumn in Williamsburg
*In Williamsburg, the people are always friendly, and the history is rich. It's another of my favorite places, and I love it year-round.*

# THE TOYMAKER

*Lantern Skaters*
(Right) The lantern's glow
created beautiful reflections on
the ice when we were skating
at night. When it was windy,
we'd open our coats and let the
wind sail us across the pond.
It felt like we were flying.

*Hand in Hand*
I've skated since the age of
three and taught our children
when they were about the same
age. In this painting, I recall
teaching Hope to skate.

When I was about ten or eleven years old, I remember my father occasionally taking me and one of my brothers or sisters to his office. It was right in the center of town, and if we went with him a few days before Christmas, we knew we'd be going Christmas shopping. It was one of the best days of December. We took all the money we'd saved and made a mental list of what Mum would love and Dad liked. Then would come the rest of the family, three brothers and three sisters.

The five-and-ten-cent store was our shopping mecca. Most of the time we bought simple things and what we could afford. Even in those days, three dollars wasn't a lot of money for eight presents. We really did some heavy thinking and made some major decisions. I remember the time my mother was really happy that I gave her a pot holder, and my dad was delighted with a box of licorice.

I think now how important it was to me that they liked what I gave them. At that age you didn't get the chance to give your parents many things, so when you did, it really meant a lot. Of course, if I had a

penny left over, I liked to buy some penny candy for myself. If I had
an extra one, I'd treat my shopping partner, too.

A couple of weeks before the actual day, decorations would start
appearing in school, at home and in town. You listened to Christmas
carols ringing out from many of the shops, and sometimes you
sang along. The event sign in town announced the coming of
*The Nutcracker*, the wonderful music- and dance-filled story
that I enjoy to this day.

The chill in the air felt that much chillier, and when snow
fell, our spirits soared. As Christmas got closer, everything got
busier. Hustle and bustle was everywhere, a delicious excitement
building toward *the day*.

The favorite place to stop and wish was the toy-maker's shop. The big wooden soldier stood as guard and friend to all who passed by year-round. Just looking through those windows was almost as good as going inside. From the outside, where you might stop on the way to go skating or sledding, you could see toys, drums, games, trains, books and puppets, and just wish your heart away. Going inside was to hear the drums, music boxes and whistles. You could smell the pinecones and Christmas tree; you could touch the hockey sticks and even open a book. My favorite wish of all was my dream of getting some toy soldiers, and one year the wish came true. I treasured them for years, and that gift

### Christmas at Bedford Falls
*(Previous pages) This is a gift to my son Joe, who loves Christmas as much as life itself. His first words on his first Christmas were "bright lights." Today he is a playwright. God has truly blessed me, and I thank Him, saying "It is a wonderful life."*

### Christmas Carousel Pony
*(Left) The wreath symbolizes eternity, and the candles, hope and love. Every item here brings a special memory to mind.*

### The Toymaker

(Above) Joseph Thomas Hope is the toymaker. Once I asked my small children if they could draw Christmas. Joe drew a lit candle; Hope, an angel guarding the Baby's manger; and Tom, a tree with lots of presents. This is in honor of what Christmas really is: the giving spirit of love and life.

### A *Christmas Morning*

The door's open just a crack for taking a peek, in case Santa hasn't left yet. In no time it will be Christmas morning in so many homes. Gifts will be opened, happy voices will be heard and smiles will abound. Rewards for being good all year will be realized and treasured.

*A Christmas Door*
(Above) I find lots of doors
interesting, and I like to design
and decorate them myself on
occasion. In this painting, I liked
the door, so I decorated it.

### Season's Greetings
*Once more I am in Colonial Williamsburg, picturing what a Christmas greeting might have been like long ago.*

### Winter Memories
*(Far right) These skates are too beautiful to be hiding in the attic. I decided to put them with the lighted lantern. Since we usually had a cup of cocoa after skating, I added the Hershey's cup. The flowers are simply a natural touch of mine.*

has always reminded me that wishes, hopes and dreams *can* come true.

Joseph Thomas Hope was the toymaker's name. It has always seemed to me that it was a wonderful thing to be a toymaker in that time, in that place. We were a villageful of kids all known personally by the man whose loving, skillful hands could create the toys each of us was wishing for. His heart and happiness were reflected in all the gifts he made or obtained. His joy was seen in the warm spirit he shared with everyone, all year round, but especially at Christmas, when his work of making people happy made his Christmas happiest of all.

*Summer Gate*
*(Detail) Hollyhocks, one of my*
*all-time favorite flowers, grow*
*straight, tall and beautiful next*
*to the white arbor. They make*
*a lovely garden even lovelier as*
*they stand guard at the gate.*

# About the Artist

There was a time when there were great art expositions in Paris, London and even this country. Before the paintings were displayed for the public, the artists were allowed to view their own creations. If they felt that here or there an area could be improved upon, they could touch up and revarnish those areas. This became known as Varnishing Day. An artist sometimes worked on a painting for over two years; some were so large that they could never get through the doorway of a normal home—not that size has anything to do with excellence, but it seldom goes unnoticed. Sometimes these improvements were necessary because gallery lighting was different from studio light. The awards of prize money and grants could greatly help an artist to continue painting without financial worries, so it was important to be shown at one's best.

Now, at the same time that an artist might be putting the touches on his own work, he could meander through the galleries to eye the competition. Gradually the artist took to arriving with not only his varnish, but maybe a couple tubes of paint and a brush or two. Maybe a touch here and there would impress the judges. As time passed, the entire procedure intensified even more, with some artists bringing an entire palette of color along. It is said that the great English landscape artist Turner included a step ladder in his equipment, as he was short in stature, and would actually repaint the whole painting *in frame!*

Times have changed and the great, big shows have diminished, as have the grants that went with them. Today, painters must find other ways of supporting themselves and their families until they reach their dreams as successful artists. Some do illustrations and the graphic arts, which was my experience. The concept of painting a picture has changed, too, including all the -isms from abstract to fool-the-eye realism. There is something for everyone. Techniques of applying paint have also changed from thick to thin, glazing to palette knife, from varied brush strokes to slick as glass, and even the power-driven airbrush. Come to think of it, I use all of the above, except the airbrush, and sometimes all in a single work. Technique is simply a means to an end—the end being to make a particular expression of a subject or an idea.

Knowledge of your subject is as important to painting as technique. In this regard, my career could be considered to have begun quite early. I grew up with many of the characters and places that appear in my paintings. The time spent on the sea has allowed me to know its many moods; the time in the garden has given me a keen awareness of the serene quality found in the abundance of life, my family, a sense of home. The keen observer will note that "J.T. Hope" is a name that finds its way into a number of my paintings. It is actually a combination of the names of all my children: Joseph, Thomas and Mary Hope.

It was at the age of seventeen that I took the first real steps toward my current career. I had gained an apprenticeship as a photoengraver for the paper I used to deliver as a child. From there it was on to the Nova Scotia College of Art, where the decision to pursue this path really took hold. Back then, New York City was the center of the art world in North America, so I left Nova Scotia for the big city and attended the Art Students League. After a brief return home to paint the sea and the people who made their living from it, I entered the world of commercial art and took a job as a photoengraver and illustrator in the Midwest.

The eastern seaboard was where my interest truly lay, and it wasn't long before I moved east to New England, where I still live today. Back then, Famous Artists Schools, founded by some of the greatest illustrators ever, were operating out of Westport, Connecticut. I became a teacher there, and that experience eventually was essential in the creation of my first book, *On Drawing and Painting*. During all of this, my true desire was to paint full-time. One day, I finally made

*Memories*
*(Detail) Molly was my dear friend, in and out of the studio. When I took a garden break to relax for a short time, she would be right next to me. Molly was as beautiful, gentle and patterned as only calicos are.*

## Joey
*Our son Joey, wearing a prized gift from his grandmother. This young spirit is ready to leap off the bench and into action.*

## Nature Entices Pleasure
*(Above right, detail) While exploring a country road in Nova Scotia, I came across this beautiful waterfall.*

## New England Landscape
*My children loved to walk rock walls, and this happy memory was painted years ago for them. I see paintings everywhere I go, and, fortunately for me, New England has so many scenes to offer.*

the decision to do just that and have been at it ever since.

Over the years, one of the most-asked questions from people has been how I go about painting a picture and how long it takes. Both questions are easy to answer. I try to paint as simply as possible. My idea is more important to me than the mechanics of the painting. How long does it take? Not long, usually. It takes longer to think through the idea than to paint it. For example, take a look at *The Flower Barn*. I saw this barn near the side of the road, not far from my home, five or six years before I painted it. It had seen better days before nature took over. I shot a few photos and made some notes for reference. I thought it had possibilities; I pondered it over the years and then conceived the idea of making a *flower* barn out of it. Now I was excited. I took a trip back to the barn, but there, in its place, a huge house was being built. Well, that's progress, I suppose. I was glad to have the photos and notes taken six years earlier.

In actually painting the subject, I decided to spruce it up and add the flowers. I thought that if there were flowers around, maybe the neighbors would want to buy them. Any self-respecting barn is a workplace, after all. So there would be someone there to collect the flowers and sell them, and instead of sitting on the porch, the rocker would be next to the barn door. After six years, it took me less than a week to paint it.

In my painting procedures, I do little or no preliminary sketching, and by "little" I mean just a thumbnail or two. I start to paint very broadly and simply, establishing only the major shapes and values. Once that's laid in, it is easier for me to see my subject in abstract terms, objectively. This is the most important part in picture-making. In it lies the strength of the composition, how the major shapes and emphases relate to each other. I try to hold back on the detail: that is the icing on the cake and comes later. So I work the whole picture, relating color and the light and dark values and shapes of the structure, never one area at one time.

Overall, in my paintings I try to create an invitation to you to recall a special memory of your own. From what I hear, most people know exactly where a place was or is and have a story of their own to tell. Some wish they could actually go into those images of mine. The most common description of my work is "peaceful." If you find a few moments of peaceful pleasure in this world as you view my paintings, thank you for accepting my invitation. I hope that they bring you as much pleasure as they give me in painting them.

*Seaside Cottage*
Like the craftsmen who built these cottages, I put the same loving care into mine.

# List of Paintings